THE BOOK OF
OF
HERBS
& SPICES

THE BOOK OF HERBS & SPICES

❧

ARABELLA BOXER
CHARLOTTE PARRY-CROOKE

CONTENTS

This edition published in 1989 by
The Hamlyn Publishing Group Limited,
a division of the Octopus Publishing Group,
Michelin House, 81 Fulham Road, London SW3 6RB.

ISBN 0 600 56472 X

Produced by Mandarin Offset.
Printed and bound in Hong Kong.

The text and illustrations are based on material which
originally appeared in *The Encyclopedia of Herbs and
Spices,* published by Octopus Books Limited.

Illustrations by Claire Davies, Jenny Mitchell and
Delyth Jones

Cover illustration by Norman Messenger

PLANNING A HERB GARDEN

One basic decision has to be made before even starting to plan a herb garden: is it to be formal or informal? Your decision will be guided partly by the space at your disposal, and partly by personal preference. There is little point in planning a formal garden within an irregular-shaped piece of land, or on uneven ground. A garden based on geometric designs demands a square, or at least rectangular, plot, and one that is perfectly flat: the garden of a small terrace house would be ideal. In fact the idea of imposing intricate geometric designs on herbs, surely the most vigorous and unruly of growing plants, may not seem entirely appropriate, yet no one would deny that herbs do look at their best growing near stone, or set against a formal hedge of clipped box or yew. Perhaps a design based on a square or rectangle, intersected with paths of stone or brick, is the perfect compromise. Once this formal design has been achieved, the herbs may be allowed to grow naturally, mingling with each other in an unforced manner. This also solves the problem of maintenance, as truly formal herb gardens must be rigorously kept up if they are to look their best. In the garden plan on the next page, the herbs have been selected for culinary purposes, although many have a decorative value too.

When siting the herb garden, remember that a sunny, sheltered spot is imperative, for almost all herbs need a few hours of sunshine each day, and dislike the wind. The herb garden should be as close to the kitchen as possible, for easy access is vital if the herbs are to be used to any great extent in cooking.

Once this has been established, a few other points should be borne in mind:

1. Plants that spread or cross-fertilize
Mints have a spreading root system that tends to take over the garden, and they cross-fertilize with each other when grown too close. Horseradish also has a creeping root system, and like mint should be planted in a container of some sort, either above or below the ground. Fennel and dill tend to cross-fertilize with each other, and should be kept apart.

2. Patterns of growth
Most herbs are perennial, but some are annuals, or best treated as such. (This applies to many of the biennials, which produce woody stems and flower-heads only during the second year.) Perennials and annuals should be mixed, when height permits, in order to avoid ugly gaps in winter. Try also to place evergreens judiciously for the same reason, to provide interest during the dormant season.

3. Contrasts in leaf, shape and colour
Much of the charm of herbs lies in the diversity of their leaves, and best use should be made of these whenever possible. Soft, downy, round leaves should be planted next to spiky needles; pale, dappled shades of white and cream against dark glossy evergreens; shiny purples and bronzes adjacent to furry silvery-greys.

4. Inclusion of flowers

Most of the visual interest of herbs lies in their leaves; with a few obvious exceptions, like bergamot, borage, rosemary and chives, their flowers are undistinguished and the herbs are picked before they have a chance to bloom. You may wish to add a few flowers, which from medieval times have been traditionally included in herb and kitchen gardens. In the Middle Ages border carnations (called gilly flowers), lilies, marigolds and violets were included. Roses were often planted in the monastic herb gardens of medieval France, and lavender earned its place as a herb for strewing on floors, and for scenting linen. More recent horticultural developments also seem appropriate today in the herb garden, for example sweet-scented geraniums and nasturtiums, whose leaves and flowers can be used in the kitchen, and pansies, a hybrid of the old-fashioned violet, which was often candied for decoration. Vines or hops seem appropriate in a walled garden, as do old-fashioned climbing roses, honeysuckle, or clematis.

1. Clematis
2. Spearmint
3. Marjoram
4. Lemon Thyme
5. Lily (*L. regale*)
6. Chervil
7. Chives
8. Lovage
9. Dill
10. Pansies
11. Common Thyme
12. Rosemary
13. Marigolds
14. Parsley
15. Tarragon
16. Border carnation
17. Basil

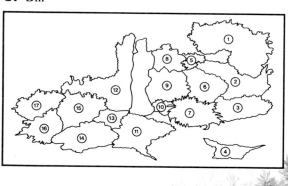

5. Inclusion of vegetables

It is hard to draw any clear line between vegetables and herbs. Celery can be included, for the sake of its leaves, as can spring onions and garlic. If there is room, one might be tempted to include more; globe artichokes add interest to any bed, as do ornamental cabbages, on a smaller scale.

The semi-formal garden needs paths, both for the sake of the overall design, and for practicality. Any bed over 90 cm (3 feet) wide also needs stepping-stones set within it, for the herbs to be within easy reach. The stones will soon be hidden from sight by the herbs themselves, but their position is easily memorized, for use in muddy weather. Ideally, paths and stepping-stones should be of grey York stone – old flag-stones or paving stones are ideal – or of old brick. Pockets of low herbs may be grown among them, in small gaps, or in the joins. Since both stone and brick are expensive, cheaper alternatives may have to be considered; concrete may be set in slabs, to resemble stone, or blocks of composition or synthetic stone may be used. An alternative is to make paths of creeping herbs, and to set pieces of stone within them, at intervals of about 45 cm (18 inches), so that they are usable even in wet weather. There are many prostrate herbs suitable for paths – various mints, thymes, and camomile – but they must be enclosed in some way to stop them encroaching on the beds. Small pieces of slate, set on edge, or small stones

make a decorative border that will take up the minimum of space.

In any formal design a centrepiece is required, as a focal point. There are many possibilities, depending on the available space, the aspect and personal preference. An irregular shape would offset the formality of the general design well. Any small tree would look good: a fruit tree grown on the least vigorous root stock, a (weeping) willow-leaf pear, a mulberry, medlar or quince. For a smaller space, a weeping standard rose would be suitable, or a honeysuckle or clematis trained as a standard.

A small statue would also look elegant as a centre-piece, or an urn filled with ivy-leafed geraniums or nasturtiums, trailing over the edge. For those who prefer a strictly geometric design, an ornamental bay tree can be grown in a tub, clipped into a pyramid shape. If the garden is itself enclosed within a wall, as in a town garden, a seat may be placed at the end; if set within a larger garden, however, as in the country, it is better to leave it open, to allow the paths to continue without interruption to the outer world.

STORING HERBS

Harvesting home-grown herbs

All herbs should be harvested at the same moment in their life cycle, after the flower buds have formed, and before they burst into bloom. They can, of course, be picked at other times, but this is when the main crop should be taken, when the foliage is at its most abundant, and the flavour most intense. After flowering, most of the strength goes into producing seeds, and – in some cases – woody stems, and the flavour grows weaker. This also applies to biennials which are in their second year of growth.

Choose a warm, dry day for harvesting and be sure to pick the herbs in the morning, after the dew has evaporated, and before the sun has reached its zenith. Annuals are best demolished and dug up, since there is little point in leaving bare, unsightly stems. Most biennials can be treated in the same way, although a few plants can be left to self-seed. In the case of perennials, the picking must

be done with care, so as not to denude the plant, and weaken it. At least one-third of the leaves must be left unpicked. Herbs that need pruning, such as bay, rosemary, and lemon verbena, will probably have already supplied enough leaves for household use at the time of pruning, which is usually done in early spring.

Drying home-grown herbs
The traditional method of storing home-grown herbs for winter use is by drying, but this is only effective in the case of a few plants whose essential oils are not too volatile to survive the drying process. Woody perennials like rosemary, bay and thyme, dry well, but as they are evergreen, the leaves may equally well be left on the shrub, and picked as needed through the winter. Both bay and rosemary require pruning to keep in shape, as does lemon verbena, and the clippings can be dried and hung in the kitchen. Most annuals are not worth drying, since their essential oils are volatile, and the flavour is lost; this applies to chervil, dill, chives, basil and parsley, as well as to the perennial tarragon. The herbs that dry best are lovage, marjoram, mint, sage and savory.

The best way to dry herbs is to lay them in a single layer, on a ventilated rack covered with a piece of muslin, in a dry, airy room. Leave them until completely dry: this may take anything from two days for delicate leaves like mint, to a week for woody herbs like rosemary. The process can be accelerated slightly by placing the rack in an airing cupboard or on a night storage heater. Branches of rosemary and bay may be hung singly and left to dry naturally. The disadvantage of drying herbs in bunches, which was common at one time, is that the air does not always penetrate right into the centre.

Once dried, the herbs become brittle. In almost all cases the leaves should be rubbed off the stalks and packed into jars. There is no need to reduce the leaves to powder, as is usually done commercially. A few, like rosemary and thyme, may be left on sprigs, for easy removal after cooking, and packed in plastic bags. If the dried herbs are stored in plain glass jars or plastic bags, they must be kept in cupboards, away from the light. Coloured glass or china jars may be left in the daylight. All containers must be carefully labelled.

Herbs dried at home have more flavour than bought ones; even so, they are best used within six months.

Freezing home-grown herbs
Most of the herbs that do not dry well can be frozen. This applies to all the delicate annuals; chervil, dill and basil, as well as to chives, parsley and tarragon. It is very simple to do; in the case of large-leafed herbs like basil, simply pick the leaves off the stalks and pack, twelve at a time, into small polythene bags, label, and freeze. With small-leafed herbs like tarragon, chervil and dill, it is better to freeze small sprigs, also packed into bags. Chives are packed in bunches, and parsley heads loosely bundled into larger polythene bags.

ANGELICA

Angelica archangelica

This impressive biennial grows to over 180 cm (6 feet) in height, with hollow stems, large, indented leaves and greenish-yellow flowers appearing from June to August in its second year. Angelica originated in Iceland, Greenland and northern Russia, but has become naturalized throughout much of Europe, including the UK.

Uses: Leaves, stems and flowers all have a sweet scent and flavour. The stem is the part most often used in the kitchen where its sweetening properties enable the cook to reduce the sugar content of the recipe. The stem is also candied, for decorating cakes and trifles, and can be bought in this form. The leaves can be chopped and added to salads.

To grow: On account of its height, angelica should always be planted at the very back of the herb garden, or separately in a large tub. It likes a light, rich, fairly damp soil, and thrives in semi-shade. It dies after flowering, but its life may be prolonged; either by cutting off the flower heads before they have formed, or by cutting the plant down to ground level in late autumn. Alternatively, if allowed to flower, it will seed itself. Angelica can be grown from seed. Sow in late summer in the position where it is to flower and thin out the seedlings to 15 cm (6 inches) apart.

BASIL

Ocimum basilicum

Sweet basil grows about 45 cm (18 inches) high, with large, lettuce-green leaves and creamy-white flowers. It originated in India, where it is perennial; in cooler countries like the UK it is best treated as a semi-hardy annual. Bush Basil (Ocimum minimum) is a lower, more compact plant with small leaves, easier to grow. Dark Opal is a decorative red-leafed variety.

Uses: Basil has a unique flavour, closely related to its fragrance. It is lost on prolonged heating, since the oil is volatile, so basil should be used only as a flavouring/ garnish, cut into strips and added to hot dishes at the end of the cooking. Basil has a special affinity with tomatoes, soft cheeses, pasta, vegetable soups and creamy sauces.

To grow: Basil is delicate, not easily grown from seed. It needs a lot of warmth to bring out its true flavour, and is best grown under glass, or on a sunny window sill, until midsummer, when it can be moved to a sheltered corner of the garden. In autumn it is best moved indoors again, where it will flourish up until Christmas, or later. Flower heads should be picked out as they form.

BAY

Laurus nobilis

Also called Sweet Bay, or Bay Laurel, this must not be confused with the common laurel (Prunus laurocerasus), whose leaves are poisonous. Bay is an evergreen and originated in the Mediterranean. It can be grown as a bushy shrub, trimmed into decorative shapes, or allowed to grow into a tree, when it may reach from 6-18 m (20-60 feet). It has glossy, dark green leaves, sometimes with wavy edges, followed by small greenish flowers in May and (sometimes) purplish black berries.

Uses: The leaves must be subjected to long cooking, when they release their inimitable flavour. It is strong, and often half a leaf is enough to flavour a dish. Bay leaves form part of the classic bouquet garni, and are almost always included in stocks, casseroles, pâtés and *court bouillons*. The leaves can be used fresh or dried, so that they may be left on the tree, or picked at any time.

To grow: Bay is a half-hardy plant, and should always be protected from the frost. Bay can be grown from cuttings, but is hard to grow from seed. If grown in a tub, it can be moved indoors in harsh weather.

BERGAMOT

Monarda didyma

This is the Red Bergamot, sometimes called Beebalm. (There are other varieties, with pink, white, or purple flowers.) It is a beautiful aromatic plant growing 90-120 cm (3-4 feet) tall, with highly scented leaves which attract the bees. Crimson flowers appear in July and August, making it a welcome addition to the herb garden.

Uses: Bergamot's culinary uses are few, but its strongly aromatic leaves make it an obvious choice for a scented garden, or bee garden. The leaves can be chopped and added to salads, while the flowers may be crystallized, for decorating iced sponge cakes.

To grow: Bergamot likes a fairly rich, moist soil, so long as it does not become water-logged, in partial or full sun. It can be reproduced by root division, in spring or autumn, and the whole plant should be divided every two or three years.

BORAGE

Borago officinalis

Borage is an annual, growing between 90-120 cm (3-4 feet) high, with large, hairy leaves and bright blue, star-shaped flowers. It grew originally in eastern Europe, but is now naturalized throughout most of Europe and North America.

Uses: Nowadays it is used mainly for its decorative features. Stems complete with leaves and flowers are the traditional garnish for Pimms and other summer cups. Both leaves and flowers have a refreshing, cucumber-like flavour. The young leaves may be added to salads, while the older leaves can be boiled or steamed like spinach, or dipped in batter and deep-fried.

To grow: Borage likes a light, fairly rich soil and a sheltered, sunny position. Like bergamot, borage attracts bees.

BOUQUET GARNI

The classic French flavouring for stocks, soups, stews and *court bouillons*, indeed, almost any dish of fish or meat which requires long, slow cooking in liquid, a bouquet garni consists of a bay leaf, a sprig of thyme and three sprigs of parsley. It is always removed after cooking, and is sometimes tied within a celery stalk or wrapped in a piece of muslin for easy removal. Other herbs such as celery, garlic and fennel can be added for specific dishes, but this is the basic mixture.

CELERY LEAVES

Apium graveolens

Celery grows wild in most parts of the world. The cultivated variety was introduced to Britain in the late seventeenth century. It is a biennial, growing between 30-45 cm (12-18 inches) high, with ridged stems, light green leaves and umbels of yellow flowers.

Uses: Celery leaves are some of the most useful and decorative of herbs. Their essential oil is less volatile than most, so that they can be subjected to heat or dried without losing their flavour. They are used in stuffings, braises and casseroles, and to garnish soups and salads.

To grow: A few plants should be included in the herb garden so that a handful of leaves can be picked at will. Celery likes a rich, damp soil. At the end of the first year, dig up all except one or two plants, which should be allowed to self-seed. See also: CELERY SEEDS (p 67).

CHERVIL

Anthriscus cerefolium

Chervil is a small annual, like a delicate parsley in appearance, growing to a height of 30-45 cm (12-18 inches). It originated on the borders of Europe and Asia and was probably brought by the Romans to Britain, where it later became naturalized.

Uses: Chervil has a light, subtle flavour that is equally good alone, or blended with other delicate herbs. It forms part of the classic mixture called *fines herbes*, for use in omelettes and sauces. On its own, chervil is good in bland, creamy soups, with baked or scrambled eggs, pounded into butter for serving with grilled fish, or for flavouring a velouté sauce. Its essential oil is a highly volatile one, so that it must not be subjected to prolonged cooking, or its flavour will be lost.

To grow: Chervil likes a light, well-drained soil, in a sheltered, half-shaded spot. Chervil leaves can be used when the plant is about 10 cm (4 inches) high.

CHIVES

Allium schoenoprasum

Chives are perennial, and grow in clumps about 12.5 cm (5 inches) high, with dark green tubular leaves and pretty round flowers appearing in early summer. They grow wild throughout most of the northern hemisphere, including parts of the UK.

Uses: Chives are the mildest of the onion family, with none of the bitterness of raw onions or the pungency of garlic. They cannot stand heat and must be used as a garnish, added to dishes after cooling. They make the ideal contrast, in flavour and in colour, to pale, creamy dishes like vichysoisse soup and scrambled eggs. They are good alone, on salads or cream cheeses, or combined with other herbs, as in *fines herbes*. They must be cut with a sharp knife, or with scissors, to avoid bruising. Chives cannot be dried, or even frozen very successfully.

To grow: Chives like a rich, moist soil in full sun; they also grow well indoors in pots on a sunny window sill. They respond to picking in moderation, but a proportion of fresh leaves must be left, and a dressing of fertilizer given after heavy picking. They should be lifted and divided every two or three years, in spring or autumn, or immediately after flowering.

CORIANDER

Coriandrum sativum

A hardy annual growing between 45 cm (18 inches) and 60 cm (2 feet) high, coriander looks much like flat-leafed parsley. To dispel confusion, rub the leaves, for both the leaves and unripe seeds of coriander give off a distinctive, some say unpleasant, smell, which disappears on cooking or drying. Coriander originated on the eastern shores of the Mediterranean, and has been cultivated for centuries throughout Asia.

Uses: The fresh leaves are chopped and added to curries and other spiced dishes, usually towards the end of the cooking, or as a garnish. They are added to stir-fried dishes, or pounded with garlic and chillies in fresh chutneys and curry paste.

To grow: It can be grown either in a sunny spot in the garden, or indoors in pots on a sunny window sill, by planting the whole coriander seeds, which are easily available, being one of the most commonly used in making curries. See also: CORIANDER SEEDS (p 72).

CURRY LEAVES

Murraya koenigii or *Chalcas koenigii*

These should not be confused with the silvery-grey leaves of the curry plant that is often grown in herb gardens for purely decorative reasons. Curry leaves are small, shiny and evergreen, slightly like small bay leaves. They grow on a tree native to southern Asia.

Uses: Curry leaves are usually chopped and fried in oil, at the start of making curry. They quickly turn brown and become crisp, when the other ingredients are added. The dried leaves may also be ground to a powder and used in making curry powder and paste. They are usually combined with garlic, chillies, ginger, coriander, and sometimes lemon grass. Like bay leaves, they can be used fresh or dried.

To grow: Not often found in British nurseries, the tree is easily grown and decorative, with an exotic, spicy fragrance.

DANDELION

Taraxacum officinale

Wild dandelions grow all over our lands, but the cultivated variety, with its broad leaves and mild flavour, is infinitely superior for eating. The bitterness of wild leaves may be reduced by blanching the whole plant; this is done by covering it with an inverted flower pot, or two slates propped up against each other, for a week to ten days before picking.

Uses: Young dandelion leaves, picked in spring or early summer, may be eaten raw in salads. They can be used alone or mixed with other leaves. (Dandelion and sorrel make a particularly good combination.) The older leaves may be picked later in the year and cooked like spinach. They may be eaten hot, or after cooling, as in Greece, dressed with olive oil and lemon juice.

DILL

Anethum graveolens

A hardy annual growing from 45 cm (18 inches) to 90 cm (3 feet) high, dill resembles fennel in that both have hollow stems, feathery leaves and umbels of yellow flowers. It is a native of Asia and eastern Europe, but is now naturalized in much of western Europe, although not in the UK.

Uses: Dill leaves have a very volatile essential oil and must not be subjected to prolonged heat, or dried. They are best used as a flavouring/garnish, and freeze well. Dill is widely used in marinades in Scandinavia, central Europe and Russia, and in soups and sauces, salads, and with potatoes.

To grow: Dill grows best in a light, medium-rich soil, with plenty of moisture. It should not be transplanted, since this makes it burst into flower. After flowering it is of little use as a herb, since its growth then goes into woody stems. If a few plants are allowed to produce flower heads, however, the herb will self-seed. See also: DILL SEEDS (p 74).

ELDER

Sambucus nigra

This species of elder is a small deciduous tree, or large shrub, native to Europe. (Different varieties are found in Asia, and America.) It has creamy-white flowers which appear in May, followed by purplish-black berries.

Uses: Both elder flowers and berries are used in making wine. The flowers can be used to good effect in the kitchen, for they give a subtle flavour reminiscent of muscat grapes, closely allied to their fragrance. They can be dipped in batter and deep-fried, as is done in Austria, and eaten either as a vegetable, or as a dessert, sprinkled with caster sugar.

To grow: It is rarely necessary to grow elder in the garden, since it abounds in our woods and hedgerows. If you do decide to grow elder, it likes a sunny place in which to grow and will thrive in a good, rather moist garden soil. The bushes should be pruned in early spring or late autumn before growth starts. Elder is not suitable for growing in containers.

FENNEL

Foeniculum vulgare

Fennel is native to the shores of the Mediterranean and of the UK. It is one of the largest of herbs, often growing over 1.5 m (5 feet) high, with woody stems, fine-cut feathery leaves and umbels of yellow flowers.

Uses: The fresh leaves, with their curious taste somewhat like aniseed, are chopped and added to sauces and fish dishes. The digestive properties of fennel have made it a traditional accompaniment to pork and other fatty meat dishes. The leaves do not dry well, and when fresh leaves are not available, it is better to use the seeds as a flavouring agent.

To grow: Easily grown, fennel likes a sunny position. It should not be grown close to dill, or they may cross-pollinate. It can be increased by root division, or allowed to self-seed. See also: FENNEL SEEDS (p 75).

FINES HERBES

This mixture of herbs is basic to the classic cuisine of France. It consists of equal parts of chervil, tarragon, parsley and chives, although occasionally other herbs are added, for example in southern France basil, fennel, oregano, sage and saffron are often included. Sometimes even chopped truffle is included as well. The well-balanced flavour of *fines herbes* can be best appreciated in an omelette, and the blend is ideal for a herb sauce.

GARLIC

Allium sativum

Garlic is a perennial bulb, with leaves growing about 30 cm (12 inches) high, and delicate pale flowers. One of the best varieties is the pink-skinned garlic which grows in Provence and Italy, available in early summer as fresh, juicy bulbs.

Uses: These are very extensive and defined by personal taste. Garlic may be eaten raw, pounded into pungent sauces or simmered in water to make the Spanish *sopa del ajo*. Whole bulbs may be divided into cloves and roasted around a joint of lamb, or slivers of garlic inserted into the surface of the meat; the longer garlic cooks, the milder the flavour. Garlic butter is delicious when spread on crusty French bread.

To grow: Garlic is easily grown by dividing into cloves which should be planted 2.5 cm (1 inch) deep and 15 cm (6 inches) apart, in late winter/early spring. If grown near fruit trees, especially peaches, garlic helps to prevent leaf curl. The cloves will thrive via rich, moist garden soil and sunny position, and the plants should be kept well-watered. In late summer, when the tops are down, lift the garlic and leave it to dry out thoroughly under cover.

GERANIUM, SWEET-SCENTED

Pelargonium

Sweet-scented geraniums, or Pelargoniums, to give them their proper name, are half hardy hybrids. They make delightful additions to the herb garden, adding both scent and colour, while their scented leaves may be used in the kitchen. There are numerous different varieties; some of the best from the culinary aspect are as follows: Pelargonium fragrans (nutmeg-scented); P. crispum and P. citriodorum (lemon-scented), P. odoratissimum (apple-scented); and P. tomentosum (peppermint-scented).

Uses: The leaves can be used to flavour a sorbet or granita, by infusing them for 20-30 minutes in a thin sugar syrup. After straining, the syrup is sharpened with lemon juice, and frozen to a mush. For a sorbet, beaten egg whites are folded in halfway through the freezing process. Pelargonium flowers may be crystallized.

To grow: Pelargoniums are easily grown from stem cuttings. These should be about 15 cm (6 inches) long, dusted with rooting powder, and planted in pots in potting compost. The best time is March or April, although it can also be done in late summer, or early autumn. They take about six weeks to root. Alternatively, they can be grown from seed, or from root cuttings. Both seed and cuttings do best at a temperature of 12-15°C (55-60°F). Do not let the compost dry out but do not overwater.

GINGER

Zingiber officinale

Ginger is a perennial plant about 90 cm (3 feet) high. It grows like a reed and has spiky green leaves and mauve and yellow flowers. Ginger originated in the jungles of tropical Asia, but has been cultivated for centuries in China, India, West Africa and the West Indies.

Uses: In the West, ginger is best known in its dried powdered form, as a spice, for flavouring cakes and biscuits, and as one of the constituents of curry powder. In the East, however, it is more widely used fresh; the rhizome is peeled, then sliced, chopped, grated or ground to a paste and used to flavour dishes of fish, chicken and meat.

To grow: Ginger is a tropical plant, and although it can be grown in this country it will not produce rhizomes. See also: GINGER (p 78).

HOPS

Humulus lupulus

Like other vines, hops are perennial, growing from 5.4-7.5 m (18-25 feet) each season. They die back to ground level each winter, then produce new shoots in the spring. They are native to Europe and western Asia, and grow wild in the UK. In the sixteenth century the cultivation of hops in this country began, and has continued ever since.

Uses: In the UK, hops are used solely for brewing, but in France, Belgium and Germany the young shoots are much esteemed as a vegetable, boiled or steamed, like asparagus. They are served hot, with a melted butter sauce, or with poached eggs; in Germany they are also eaten cold, as a salad. Unless grown in private gardens, hops are unobtainable in the UK, since the ones in general cultivation have been sprayed, and are unfit for consumption.

To grow: Three hop vines, trained up a tripod of 180 cm (6 foot) bamboo poles, make a decorative feature for a herb garden, especially in midsummer when the 'cones' appear. These are the female flowers, or bracts. Hops should be planted in rich soil, in an open sunny spot.

HORSERADISH

Cochlearia armoracia

A hardy perennial with wavy, indented leaves and tiny white flowers, horseradish grows 60-90 cm (2-3 feet) high, and has a thick, buff-coloured tap root. It originated on the borders of Europe and Asia and has been cultivated in the UK since the sixteenth century.

Uses: The root is grated and used as a condiment, in much the same way as mustard. In the UK it is the traditional accompaniment to roast beef. When not available fresh, it can be bought ready grated, or in the form of a creamy sauce; much the best produce is one preserved with citric acid, imported from Germany or Scandinavia. Horseradish can be combined with mustard in a sauce for fish, chicken, eggs or vegetables, or with stewed apples in a sauce for duck or goose.

To grow: The horseradish root grows deep and spreads laterally. It likes a light, rich, well-manured soil and an open sunny position. Sections of root can be planted in the spring and dug up the following autumn, by which time they will have grown into a sizeable root.

L

LEMON BALM

Melissa officinalis

Lemon balm is a perennial growing to around 90 cm (3 feet), with aromatic leaves which give off a strong lemon fragrance when crushed. It is a native of the Mediterranean and was much grown in Britain in the Middle Ages. It produces small pinkish-white flowers in midsummer.

Uses: The leaves can be chopped and added to stuffings for poultry and game, salads, desserts and fruit cups. They have a flavour somewhat like lemon rind, but more perfumed, and can be used in recipes as a substitute for lemon grass.

To grow: Although its culinary uses are few, lemon balm is a pretty plant and eminently suitable for a scented garden, or bee garden. It likes a sheltered spot in partial shade, with fairly rich, moist soil. Propagate by root division in spring or autumn.

LEMON GRASS

Cymbopogon citratus

Lemon grass is a perennial, native to South-East Asia. It is also found in Africa, South America and Australia. It has pointed aromatic leaves, sharp and spiky, with a slightly swollen leaf base.

Uses: The lower sections of the leaves especially contain an aromatic oil with a strong lemon flavour. Lemon grass leaves are used extensively in South-East Asian curries and spiced dishes, usually in conjunction with garlic, ginger and curry leaves, or fresh coriander. The fresh leaves are peeled and sliced, or chopped, while the dried leaf can be tied in a knot and removed after cooking, like a bay leaf. The powdered form is strong and should be used sparingly.

To grow: Lemon grass is easily grown in pots, if you can manage to get hold of a root.

LEMON VERBENA

Lippia citriodora

Also called Lemon-scented verbena, this is a pretty shrub with light green leaves and pale flowers in late summer. It is perennial and deciduous, and will grow to 3 m (10 feet) or more. A native of South America, it was brought to Europe by the Spaniards.

Uses: It can be used to give a lemon tang to dishes of chicken or fish, stuffings, salads, or desserts, but in moderation, as it has a rather perfumed flavour.

To grow: Grow from cuttings taken in summer. Plant in a sunny, sheltered spot, in a light, well-drained soil. Lemon verbena needs protection from frost, except in very favourable positions. Since it is deciduous, it can be cut back to ground level in winter, and covered with garden compost or bracken. Alternatively, prune the plant in spring.

LOVAGE

Levisticum officinalis

Lovage is a hardy perennial growing over 120 cm (4 feet) high, with large, dark green leaves. It is a native of the Mediterranean but has become naturalized in parts of the UK.

Uses: At one time lovage used to be blanched and cooked like celery, and eaten as a vegetable, while the stems were candied like those of angelica. Nowadays, lovage is not much used, even as a herb. It deserves a place in the herb garden, however, for it is a handsome plant and yields a generous supply of leaves with a warm, robust flavour somewhat similar to celery. They preserve their flavour well, both on cooking and drying, so can be used all through the winter in one form or another. The chopped leaves are good alone, or combined with other robust herbs, in stuffings, stews and soups, and in fresh tomato sauce for pasta.

To grow: Lovage is a vigorous plant, easily grown, so long as there is adequate space to accommodate it. It likes a fairly rich soil, either in partial shade or full sun, and is best propagated by division in spring or autumn.

MARIGOLD

Calendula officinalis

This is the old-fashioned pot marigold, a hardy annual traditionally grown in herb gardens or kitchen gardens. A native of southern Europe, the marigold grows wild throughout the British Isles. It produces its single yellow flowers from June until October.

Uses: The flower-heads are used fresh in salads, or dried, in soups and meat stews. They add both flavour and colour and have been used in the past as a substitute for saffron, in rice and fish dishes, cakes and puddings.

To grow: Sow in March or April in drills in light, rich soil and a sunny position, and thin out to 30 cm (12 inches) to allow them to spread. Marigolds will also self-seed, if some flower-heads are left on the plants.

MARJORAM, SWEET
Origanum majorana

Three main varieties of marjoram are grown in the UK, but sweet marjoram is the most important for use in cooking. In its native Mediterranean, marjoram is a perennial, but in our harsher climate it is treated as an annual, growing about 30 cm (12 inches) high. Pot, or French marjoram (Origanum onites), also native to the Mediterranean, is hardier, and grows as a perennial even in the UK, forming a compact bush up to 60 cm (2 feet) high. This is the same herb as the Italian oregano, and the Greek *rigani*, but its flavour varies widely.

Uses: Sweet marjoram is best used fresh to flavour spicy meat dishes, marrow and potatoes, while dried oregano goes exceptionally well with tomatoes.

To grow: Sweet marjoram is delicate and is best sown under glass, then transplanted into a sunny corner after all danger of frost is over.

MINT

BLACK PEPPERMINT
Mentha piperita vulgaris

Decorative, with purple stem, veined leaves and mauve flowers. It grows 90 cm (3 feet) high. The leaves have a menthol-scented oil.

BOWLES' MINT

M. rotundifolia

Largest of all the mints, this grows 1.5 m (5 feet) high, with soft, downy leaves.

CORSICAN MINT

M. requienii

A tiny plant, not more than 2.5 cm (1 inch) high. Ideal for paths, with minute mauve flowers, and a peppermint scent when crushed.

EAU-DE-COLOGNE MINT

M. piperita citrata

Also called Orange mint. It has a red stem and red-veined leaves, with a sharp scent, good for pot-pourri.

PENNYROYAL

M. pulegium

Under 5 cm (2 inches) high, this mint is good for growing between paving stones. Small pink flowers and peppermint scent.

PINEAPPLE MINT

M. rotundifolia variegata

Prettiest of all the mints, this has pale green leaves dappled with cream and white, and a fresh, fruity scent and flavour.

SPEARMINT

M. spicata

The common or garden mint, best known in Britain. It grows 45-60 cm (1½-2 feet) high, with smooth, dark green leaves and small white flowers in August.

Uses: Spearmint is the mint most commonly used in the UK, for making mint sauce and jellies, and cooking with garden peas and new potatoes. Bowles' mint has a superior flavour; do not be put off by its hairy leaves. Peppermint is easily recognized by its toothpaste flavour, while Eau-de-Cologne mint and Pineapple mint are rather too perfumed for most tastes to be of any real use in cooking.

To grow: Mint is best planted in the ground in a container — a metal bucket or large tin can — as the roots spread and take over the garden. This variety is easily grown by planting runners in light, moist soil, in a semi-shaded spot.

NASTURTIUM

Tropaeolum majus

The nasturtium is actually a climbing plant, but is usually left to sprawl along the ground. It has round leaves and orange or yellow flowers, with long spurs. It is often grown in herb gardens or kitchen gardens, since the leaves, flowers, and seeds can all be used in cooking.

Uses: The leaves have a hot, peppery flavour, and can be added to salads, or bland vegetable soups as a garnish, or very finely chopped and used in sandwiches. The unripe seeds and flower buds may be pickled in vinegar and used as a substitute for capers. The flowers make a pretty addition to a green salad, or can be crystallized for decorating iced cakes.

To grow: Sow nasturtiums in well-drained soil, not too rich, in a sunny position. They grow well in window boxes and other containers.

NETTLE

Urtica dioica

Nettles grow well all over the world, wherever the climate is temperate. They are perennial, growing about 90 cm (3 feet) high, with dark green leaves and pendulous, greenish-white flowers. The leaves are covered with fine hairs containing formic acid, which gives them their sting. They spread quickly both by a creeping root system and by seed.

Uses: The young shoots of nettles, picked in spring or early summer, may be cooked and eaten like spinach, provided they have not been sprayed at any stage. Once cooked, nettles lose their sting, but protective gloves must be worn when picking them. They can be served whole or puréed.

PARSLEY

Petroselinum crispum

A hardy biennial, growing from 15-20 cm (6-8 inches) high. Parsley grew first in south-eastern Europe, near the Mediterranean, and was probably brought to Britain by the Romans.

Uses: In the UK parsley is used mainly as a garnish, but with its delicious flavour it can be used much more widely in cooking. Parsley forms part of the bouquet garni and *fines herbes* mixture. The essential oil is a volatile one, and except in the case of the bouquet garni, it should be added to food after cooking. Parsley sauce is the traditional English accompaniment to boiled bacon and poached fish. Chopped parsley may be added generously to vegetable soups, fish pies, vegetable purées and salads, while whole sprigs can be deep fried as an elegant and nutritious garnish for fish. Parsley loses its flavour when dried, but may be successfully frozen.

To grow: Parsley is troublesome to grow, being extremely slow to germinate. It should be sown in drills 25 cm (10 inches) apart, under 1 mm (⅛ inch) fine soil, and thinned out later to 15 cm (6 inches). It dislikes cold soil, so should be sown under cloches in spring, or in the open ground from May. An old gardener's tip is to water the drills with boiling water before sowing. Parsley likes a rich, well-drained soil in partial or full sun, and responds to frequent feeding. Although a biennial, it is best treated as a annual, since it produces few leaves in its second year.

PURSLANE

Portulaca oleracea

Purslane is an annual, with fleshy stalks and rosettes of green leaves. It spreads over the ground, sending up stalks 15-20 cm (6-8 inches) high, with rosettes of leaves on the tips.

Uses: The tender tips of the stalks may be eaten raw, as a salad, alone or with other leaves. Purslane can also be cooked like spinach; in Greece it is cooked with eggs, as a sort of frittata/omelette. A few fresh young purslane leaves can be included in light summer soups. Its sharp, clear flavour also blends well with bland ingredients such as cream cheese.

To grow: Purslane is easily grown from seed in the spring, in a sunny spot. It needs plenty of moisture, but the soil should be well drained.

ROCKET

Eruca sativa

Rocket is an annual, related to the mustard family. It is a native of southern Europe and was brought to Britain in the sixteenth century. It was very popular in Britain in Elizabethan times but is rarely seen nowadays in the UK, although it is still widely cultivated in France, Italy, Greece, Turkey and the USA.

Uses: The young leaves have a warm, peppery flavour, and are delicious in mixed salads. They are also good eaten alone, dressed with oil and vinegar.

To grow: Rocket is easily grown from seed. Sow from April until midsummer, in open ground, and water frequently. If allowed to become dry, the leaves will become rank and sour. Frequent picking encourages new leaf growth. Sadly, seed is hard to find in the UK, but is easily obtainable in France, Italy and the USA.

ROSEMARY

Rosmarinus officinalis

Rosemary is a bushy shrub, often growing over 180 cm (6 feet) high. It is a perennial, but being delicate, it sometimes fails to survive a hard winter. It has evergreen needles, dark green on top and silvery-grey underneath. It produces light blue flowers in early summer, which attract bees. It is native to the eastern Mediterranean.

Uses: Rosemary's essential oil is a powerful one, not especially volatile. Indeed, its flavour is so robust it can be overpowering, and should be used in strict moderation. Rosemary is best used to flavour roast and stewed mutton and lamb, or in stuffings for strongly-flavoured meat and game.

To grow: Choose a sheltered, sunny spot, preferably against a wall, or in a corner, for rosemary needs all the protection it can get. If grown in a large pot, it can be moved indoors in severe weather. Rosemary makes a good hedge, if clipped back after flowering. The clippings can be dried for use in cooking.

SAGE

Salvia officinalis

Sage is a perennial shrub with soft grey leaves, growing about 45 cm (18 inches) high. It is native to southern Europe but has been grown in Britain since the fourteenth century. The variety most commonly grown for cooking is the non-flowering broad-leaved sage.

Uses: Sage has an extremely powerful flavour and can be used fresh or dried. It does not lose its taste, even after long cooking, but tends to dominate all others. It is traditionally used to offset fatty meats, such as pork, duck and goose.

To grow: Sage grows well in a sheltered spot, in partial shade. It is only fairly hardy and may need protection during periods of hard frost. The plants should be lifted and divided every two years, after flowering. It is also easily propagated by cuttings taken from mature plants. It can be grown from seeds, but this is a lengthy process, as the plants do not mature until they are two years old. Sage tends to become somewhat straggly in late summer and should be clipped back to a tidy shape after flowering.

SALAD BURNET

Poterium sanguisorba

Salad burnet is a perennial, growing wild throughout the UK and other parts of Europe. It is a hardy plant growing about 30 cm (1 foot) high, with pretty leaflets, nine on each leaf stalk. Small green flowers with red stamens appear in late summer.

Uses: The young leaves have an appealing flavour, fresh and cool, somewhat like cucumber. They do not dry well, nor can they be subjected to heat without losing much of their flavour. They are best used as a garnish, with salads and other cold food. The flavour goes well with iced soups, tomato or cucumber salads and mousses of shellfish or eggs.

To grow: Salad burnet is easily grown from seed; sow in spring, in light, well-drained soil, and thin out later to 30 cm (12 inches) apart. Alternatively, some of the plants can be allowed to produce flower-heads, when they will self-seed. Although salad burnet is perennial, it is best to keep growing new plants as the young leaves are far more tender than the old ones.

SORREL

Rumex acetosa, R. scutatus

Sorrel, a perennial, grows in clumps. Mature plants reach 45-60 cm (18 inches-2 feet) high. It has bright green, sword-shaped leaves, with spikes of reddish flowers. Common sorrel (R. acetosa) is the variety most usually grown in the UK, but French sorrel (R. scutatus) is far superior in terms of flavour.

Uses: Raw, sorrel makes an excellent addition to mixed green salads; a few small leaves should be finely chopped and mixed through, but remember to cut down on the vinegar or lemon juice in the salad dressing. Sorrel can be cooked exactly like spinach, but having a high water content – again, like spinach – it shrinks drastically and one must allow 250 g (9 oz) per serving. It goes well with bland foods, in sauces for poached fish, as a base for poached eggs, or in hot or cold soups.

To grow: Sorrel can be grown from seed, or by root division. The plants should be lifted and divided every two or three years, then replanted in a different spot, or the flavour will deteriorate and become coarse. Sow seed in drills in April or May, in a medium-rich soil in a sunny spot, then thin out to about 20 cm (8 inches).

SPRING ONION

Allium ascalonicum

Spring onions are simply immature onions, usually a variety called White Lisbon, grown from seed and harvested before the bulb has formed.

Uses: In the UK spring onions are usually eaten raw, in salads, or with bread and cheese. Their strong flavour is milder when cooked, however, and they may be stir-fried or steamed, or used as a garnish.

To grow: Spring onions are grown from seed and dug up before they have matured.

SUMMER SAVORY

Satureia hortensis

Summer savory is an annual growing about 45 cm (18 inches) high, with narrow green leaves and small pink flowers which appear in July.

Uses: Savory is much used in France and Germany, rather in the way that sage is used in the UK. It is supposed to have an affinity with bean dishes, and is often used in conjunction with fatty meats, in pork sausages and stuffings. Savory has a strong, rather bitter flavour, and should be used in moderation. It needs long cooking to bring out and mellow its true flavour; it also dries well.

To grow: Summer savory can be grown from seed sown in April, in light, rich soil. Thin out later to 20 cm (8 inches) and do not be alarmed if it is slow to germinate. Plants will also self-seed, if allowed. Since it dries so well, it is a good idea to pick most of the plants just before they flower, in early July, and dry them for winter use, leaving a few to self-seed.

SWEET CICELY

Myrrhis odorata

Sweet cicely is a perennial growing over 90 cm (3 feet) high. It has a thick tap-root, hollow stems, and pretty fern-like green leaves. Umbels of lacy white flowers appear in May, followed by shiny brown fruits. It looks rather like a delicate cow parsley. The leaves are aromatic, with a sweet scent reminiscent of aniseed.

Uses: Like those of angelica, sweet cicely leaves have a natural sweetness and can be used to sweeten puddings that include fruits such as rhubarb, gooseberries, black-currants or plums, which may need only a subtle sweetening. They can also be chopped and added to salads and salad dressings.

To grow: Sow from seed in early spring, or propagate by root division; it will also self-seed successfully. Being a native of woodlands, sweet cicely likes moisture and shade.

TARRAGON

Artemisia dracunculus

This is the true French tarragon, not to be confused with Russian tarragon (A. dracunculoides), which looks very similar, but with coarser, virtually tasteless leaves. French tarragon is a perennial, a bushy shrub growing 75-90 cm (2½-3 feet) high, with narrow green leaves and spikes of greenish-yellow flowers in July and August.

Uses: French tarragon is one of the subtlest of herbs, and goes well with foods of delicate flavour, such as eggs, fish, chicken and veal, either alone, or mixed with other herbs. It is part of the classic *fines herbes* mixture, and is good used in sauces, and hot or cold soups. French tarragon's essential oil is volatile, but potent; it is lost when dried, but the fresh herb can be cooked, or used as a garnish. Tarragon vinegar, made by steeping the fresh herb in white wine vinegar, can be used to make summery vinaigrettes and marinades.

To grow: In cool climates like that of the UK, French tarragon produces little, if any, seed and must be grown from cuttings or by root division. Plants should be lifted every two or three years, then divided and replanted in fresh soil, for the flavour will deteriorate with age. French tarragon is only fairly hardy, and needs some protection from frost. Plant it in a warm, sheltered, sunny spot, in a well-drained, medium-rich soil. Tarragon grows well in containers.

THYME

COMMON THYME
Thymus vulgaris

This is the variety of thyme most often cultivated, growing as a bushy shrub about 30 cm (12 inches) high, with small, greyish-green, aromatic leaves and tiny mauve flowers in May and June. It is a native of southern Europe and the northern shores of the Mediterranean. There is also a golden variety with variegated leaves (T. vulgaris aureus).

CREEPING AND PROSTRATE FORMS

These include T. serpyllum 'Pink Chintz', T. Doone Valley, T. minimus, T. micromirea and many others. The flowers vary from white to crimson, pale blue to purple and are ideal for carpeting paths, banks and small lawns.

LEMON THYME
T. citriodorus

This variety has a delicate lemon flavour. There is also a golden form (T. citriodorus aureus) and a creeping lemon thyme (T. azoricus).
Uses: Common thyme is good with meat, game and in stuffings. Lemon thyme goes well with chicken and fish.
To grow: Thyme needs aridity and heat to concentrate its flavour. Thyme can be grown from seed, but it is easier to grow from cuttings, or by root division, in spring or autumn.

WILD THYME
T. serpyllum

This pretty, low-growing plant grows wild in the UK and over parts of northern Europe. The flavour is inferior to that of common thyme.

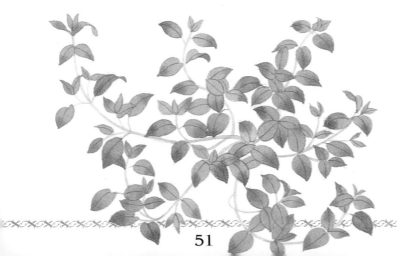

VIOLET

Viola odorata

This is the old-fashioned sweet violet which grows wild in the south of the UK and in much of Europe. It is found on the edge of woods and in hedgerows. It grows under 15 cm (6 inches) high, with dark green, heart-shaped leaves and purple or white flowers, with a strong, sweet scent. A perennial, it spreads by a system of creeping runners.

Uses: In medieval England, violets were widely used in soups, sauces, salads and desserts. Nowadays they are used almost exclusively in crystallized form for decorating desserts or cakes.

To grow: Propagate by detaching some of the creeping runners and planting in a moist shady position.

WATERCRESS

Nasturtium officinale

Watercress grows wild in the UK and in the rest of Europe, where it can be found on the banks of streams and in low-lying water meadows. It likes to grow with its roots in mud, or under water. A perennial with a spreading root system, watercress has hollow stems growing up to 30 cm (12 inches) high, with dark green leaves and tiny white flowers in midsummer. The leaves and stems, which are the edible parts, have a peppery flavour. Watercress is rich in iron and vitamin C.

Uses: Too often used merely as a garnish, watercress is a delicious and nutritious plant. It can be eaten raw in salads, or cooked like spinach and puréed. It makes excellent sauces for chicken, veal, or fish.

To grow: Since watercress is so easy to buy, it is hardly worth the trouble of growing it. In any case, this can only be done if you have a source of clean, running water nearby, and are prepared to grapple with underwater planting and muddy harvesting. Watercress can be grown from seed, then planted out on the banks of a stream, or portions of the root can be transplanted under running water, in a shallow stream bed.

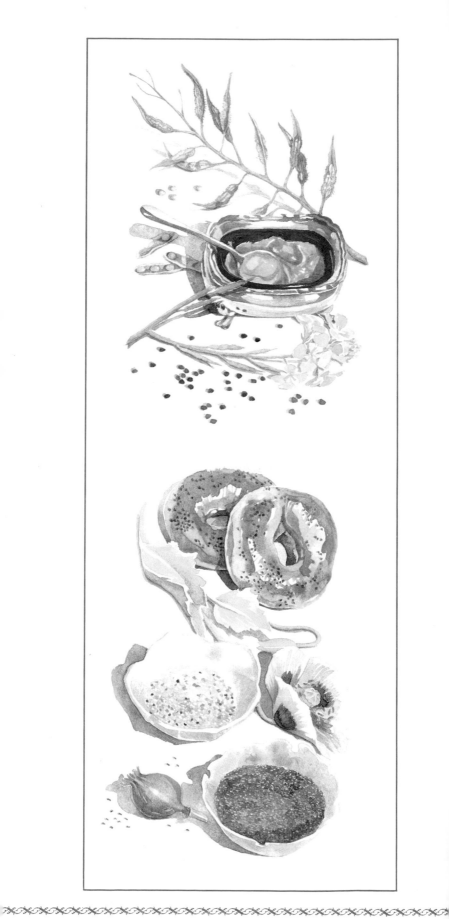

SPICES

USING WHOLE SPICES

Whole spices, stored in airtight containers, will retain their flavour much longer than those already ground. Cinnamon quills can be used whole and removed at the end of cooking, allspice and cloves can be used whole or ground as required, and nutmeg grated straight into the mixing bowl. The distinctive, sweetly aromatic flavour of coriander seeds actually improves with keeping and is released when they are pounded in a pestle and mortar. Cardamom quickly loses its unique aroma in the powdered form so buy the pods whole and crush them to release the seeds if these are needed separately.

STORING SPICES

Ready-ground, good quality spices will keep fresh for longish periods under the right conditions. It is necessary to keep the flavour in, moisture and adverse smells out and glass with an airtight top makes the best non-porous container. Polythene and cardboard can take in unwanted flavours and leak out moisture and some strong spices react with metal containers. The less they are exposed to air, the better they keep, so it is wise to buy small amounts that can be used quickly, rather than repeatedly dipping into a large jar, letting in the air each time. Never measure from a container held over a steaming pot, as the moisture can spoil the remainder of the contents.

Strong light fades the colour of some spices, particularly cayenne, paprika, chilli and saffron and spoils their special qualities, so they should not be displayed on racks in the sunniest part of the kitchen. However attractive the rack, it is far more sensible to position it on the inside of a cupboard door. If this is not possible, then use large labels on the jars and choose the coolest part of the kitchen.

AJOWAN

Carum ajowan

Ajowan is a small annual of the parsley family, closely related to cumin and caraway; it grows between 30-60 cm (1-2 feet) high. Its small, oval, reddish or greenish-brown striped seeds have a strong aroma and flavour of thyme and are used dried as a spice in parts of the Middle East and Asia, especially in their native India. Ajowan seeds are available whole or ground from Asian food shops and keep indefinitely in an airtight container.

Uses: Not much used in the West, ajowan seeds are useful for authentic Indian cooking; use them whole, lightly bruised, crushed or ground, according to recipe requirements. Occasionally a component of home-ground curry powders and other spicy mixtures, they are more frequently used in pulse dishes and in the many savouries and snacks so popular in India. Crispy, deep-fried snack dishes such as *pakoras* (small puffs of batter-coated vegetables, cheese or meat), many types of savoury biscuit, and *sev* (thin spirals of deep-fried spiced chick pea flour) often include them, as do *parathas* and *paratha* stuffings.

ALLSPICE

Pimenta dioica

Allspice berries are the small, round, dried fruit of a tall, aromatic evergreen of the myrtle and clove family, which can grow to over 12 m (40 feet). Picked when green and unripe, they are dried in the sun to a rich, deep brown colour; they are similar in size and shape to large peppercorns, though less wrinkled. Native to the West Indies and parts of Latin America, allspice grows prolifically in Jamaica where it is widely used in native dishes. Its flavour, a mingling of the tastes of cloves, cinnamon and nutmeg, with cloves predominating, gives allspice its name.

Uses: Despite its combination of oriental flavours, allspice is a favourite Western spice. It can be used in both savoury and sweet dishes; smoked and pickled foods such as raw fish, salamis and other Continental sausages are frequently flavoured with it, as are traditional English pork or game pies. A few berries are often included in meat and game marinades and winter soups. As a sweet spice it is used ground in pies, cakes and puddings, especially in Christmas pudding recipes.

AMCHUR

Mangifera indica

Amchur is unripe fruit of the mango tree, a tropical evergreen which has been cultivated in India for over 4,000 years. The mango tree can reach a height of 39 m (130 feet) and grows extensively in other tropical areas, especially South-East Asia, although amchur is associated primarily with India. The sour green mangos are sliced and dried in the sun, turning a light brown; the powder made from them is similar but a paler colour. Amchur can be bought from good Indian or Asian grocers in sliced or powdered form.

Uses: Amchur, powdered or sliced, features in a wide variety of savoury Indian dishes. Tart, with a sweet/sour taste, it is used, like tamarind, as a souring agent in curries, chutneys and pickles, and also to tenderize meat. Like lemon juice, it has a natural affinity with fish and chicken and is often included in spicy marinades for grilled or barbecued fish dishes, such as *tikkas* (fish chunks barbecued on skewers). Many fresh vegetables, aubergines and potatoes for example, are cooked with amchur, added towards the end of the cooking time.

ANISEED

Pimpinella anisum

The aromatic anise annual grows to about 60 cm (2 feet) high and is similar to other small members of the parsley family. A native of the Middle East, the plant is now established in south-eastern Europe, North Africa, India and parts of Latin America.

Uses: Aniseed's spicy/sweet flavour combines well with both sweet and savoury foods. It is used in northern and eastern Europe in confectionery, desserts, biscuits, cakes and breads. Aniseed is a favourite seasoning in Indian fish curries and marinades, the seeds are often lightly dry roasted in a frying pan before use, to bring out their full flavour. Aniseed-flavoured alcoholic drinks are often used in cooking, e.g. in Lobster à l'Anise.

ANNATTO
Bixa orellana

Annatto is a red seed, best known in the West as an orangey-red dye for food and fabric, but it is used as a spice in a number of tropical countries. Sometimes growing 10.5 m (35 feet) high, the tree's leaves and prickly fruit pods are both heart-shaped. The latter contain a mass of small, deep red triangular seeds which can be bought from West Indian grocers.

Uses: The rather peppery seeds are particularly effective with fish, rice and vegetable dishes. Annatto is used in Jamaica in a sauce for salt cod and ackee, and in the Philippines in *pipian*, a traditional dish of chicken and pork cubes braised in a spicy sauce. In Mexico annatto seeds give the characteristic colour and spiciness to stews, sauces and taco fillings. In the West the use of annatto is confined to colouring smoked fish and the rinds of cheeses such as Edam.

ASAFOETIDA
Ferula asafoetida

Asafoetida, or 'Giant Fennel', is a huge, odiferous member of the parsley family which grows to 3 m (10 feet) high and is native to the Middle East, Afghanistan and north India. It is known colloquially as 'Stinking Gum' or 'Devil's Dung' and yields an equally evil-smelling spice. The spice asafoetida is made from the sap from the plant's stems and roots, which solidifies into grey-yellow lumps which then turn a reddish-brown with a crystal-like appearance. When used in minute quantities it is a remarkable enhancer of other tastes. Do not be put off by its appearance, or indeed its frightful smell, for this disappears in cooking.

Uses: Used very occasionally in France, asafoetida is used extensively in spicy Middle Eastern vegetable dishes and in regional Indian cooking, in meat dishes like *kormas*, and in pickles, soups, vegetarian and fish dishes.

CARAWAY SEEDS

Carum carvi

The small caraway annual is a member of the parsley family and closely related to fennel and dill, both of which it resembles. It grows to between 45-60 cm (1½-2 feet) and is cultivated in many temperate regions, including parts of Europe, the southern Mediterranean and the USA. Caraway seeds are small, oval and ribbed, light to dark brown in colour. Strongly aromatic, they have a warming peppery undertone.

Uses: Caraway successfully bridges the gap between sweet and savoury foods. Germany and Austria use more caraway than any other country; the rest of northern Europe, parts of eastern Europe and Scandinavia are also large consumers. Breads such as rye and pumpernickel frequently include caraway, as do German and Austrian seed cakes, dumplings, cheeses, noodle dishes, soups and goulashes.

CARDAMOM

Elettaria cardamomum

The cardamom bush is a relative of the ginger plant and grows nearly 3 m (10 feet) high, its pod-bearing stalks sprawling along the ground. Native to India, the cardamom plant is now established in other tropical regions, including parts of Indonesia, China and Latin America. The whole seed-pod is used as the spice more often than the individual seeds it contains and three types of cardamom pod are available in the West. Most frequently seen is the small, oval, grey-green, ridged pod containing minute dark brown seeds. White cardamoms are merely bleached versions of the green, while the 'black' cardamom is actually brown and resembles a dark, hairy beetle. The aroma of cardamom is unique and unmistakable; its flavour is sweet but clean with a hint of eucalyptus. Cardamom is an expensive spice.

Uses: Cardamom is one of the essential spices in Indian food, crucial in *biryanis*, *pilaus*, *dals* and curries, particularly those of northern India. Cardamom is an important component of spice mixtures such as garam masala, and also imparts its perfumed flavour to many Indian sweet dishes and beverages.

CASSIA

Cinnamomum cassia

Cassia and cinnamon both come from the bark of closely related trees of the laurel family. The cassia of the spice trade is the bark of young shoots, sold as quills (small curled-up rolls of bark), pieces or as a powder. The rusty brown quills and pieces, about 7.5 cm (3 inches) long, are thicker, rougher and altogether less delicate than cinnamon quills. Cassia tastes and smells very much like cinnamon, but is stronger and more bitter. The pieces are usually very hard, so it is useful to have at hand both pieces and powder, stored in airtight containers. Cassia can be acquired from good grocery stores.

Uses: Cassia is frequently used in the same manner as cinnamon but for preference reserve its stronger flavour for savoury foods and leave the more delicate cinnamon for sweet dishes. Spicy Indonesian curries can be flavoured with cassia, as can those from China, where it is considered one of the great spices. Indian curries and Middle Eastern stews can be flavoured with cassia, as can an English stew or casserole – but remember to remove it before serving.

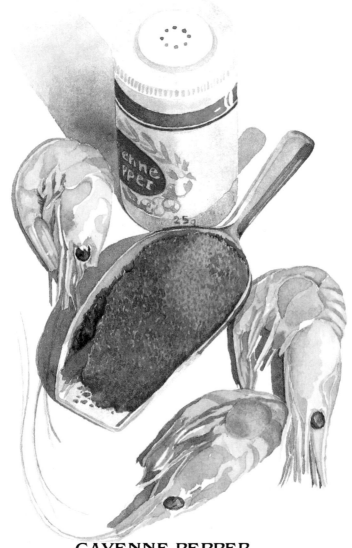

CAYENNE PEPPER

Capsicum frutescens

Cayenne pepper, paprika and Tabasco sauce are all made from varieties of capsicum, a vast collection of plants which range from small, searingly fiery chillies to the mild and much larger sweet bell pepper. Cayenne pepper is made from the flesh and seeds of the small, slender fruits of the 'Bird chilli', ripened to a bright yellow or red, dried and ground to a fine powder. Though the powerful 'heat' of cayenne is not as fierce as some chilli powders, it is nonetheless very pungent.

Uses: Cayenne pepper is used as a spice, a seasoning and a condiment, and as a milder alternative to chilli powder. It is important in Indian, North African and Latin American dishes, to which it imparts a characteristic deep red colour and rich flavour. Cayenne has an affinity with fish and seafood and is used extensively as a seasoning in lobster, crab, prawn and oyster dishes. Cayenne teams well with cheese and eggs, and is an ingredient of devil sauces and spice mixes for deep-frying chicken, fish and vegetables. See also: CHILLI (p 67), PAPRIKA (p 87).

CELERY SEEDS

Apium graveolens

Celery is a member of the parsley family, related to both fennel and dill. The plant is familiar as a salad and stew ingredient, but the narrow, grey-green, ridged, oval seeds are also used in cooking in the West. The taste and aroma of celery seeds are similar to those of the plant, but more pungent and bitter. Buy seeds whole and crush as necessary. If you grow celery, allow the plants to flower, harvest the flower-heads in the autumn of their second year and hang them upside down to dry over a container to catch their seeds.

Uses: Celery seeds are popular in English, French and American cooking, and in dishes from the Balkans. They are often used with celery sticks (to accentuate the flavour), or as a substitute for them in soups, sauces, stuffings and vegetable dishes. Celery seeds and tomatoes are natural partners in pasta sauces, rice dishes and 'Bloody Mary' cocktails. They can be included in fish soups, marinades, stocks and seafood sauces and give extra flavouring to breads and biscuits. See also: CELERY LEAVES (p 16).

CHILLI

Capsicum annuum
Capsicum frutescens

Fiery chilli 'peppers' are a very ancient spice, their cultivation stretching back 10,000 years. Chillies originate in Latin America, they belong to the capsicum branch of the plant family which numbers among its members the tomato, the potato and the aubergine. The vast variety of different types of chilli defies consistent classification and indeed description (there are over a hundred different kinds in Mexico alone!); all varieties of chilli pepper do, however, bear certain common characteristics. With a preference for tropical or sub-tropical climates, the bushy chilli shrub grows to between 30 cm-1.8 m (1-6 feet) high, depending on variety; the various plants' berries, which become the spice, all share a smooth, shiny and taut skin which protects a hollow fruit containing several fleshy ribs, a central core and numerous tiny seeds, usually white in colour. Beyond these features the similarity ends, for the different fruits vary enormously in shape, size, colour and strength. The variety most commonly seen on our market stalls and in greengrocers are small, thin and tapering red or green fruits of about 7.5-10 cm (3-4 inches) long. As a very general rule (to which, needless to say, there are exceptions), the smaller, narrower and darker the chilli, the greater its pungency.

CHILLI *(cont.)*

The chilli is a crucial and essential culinary requisite in Latin America, Indonesia, South-East Asia, China, Japan, India, the Middle East and all parts of Africa.

Many different types of fresh and dried chillies are easily acquired; one can choose between fresh unripe or ripe whole chillies, dried whole chillies, chilli powders, and chilli seasonings. Two of the best known chilli powders, cayenne and paprika, come from particular types of chilli. Chilli powder (as opposed to either of the former) is usually dried ground chillies of unspecified variety, while chilli seasoning is frequently a blend of dried ground chillies, with salt, garlic, cumin and oregano or other dried herbs.

For the unaccustomed it is better to err on the side of caution when trying and indeed preparing chillies. Wear rubber gloves during preparation and never touch eyes or mouth with fingers which have handled a hot chilli. Chilli seeds are invariably more pungent than the flesh, so discard them for less blistering results.

Uses: In many tropical areas chillies are used with the same frequency as true pepper is in Europe. Their uses are numerous and diverse and they feature daily in one form or another in the majority of local savoury dishes in the regions where they grow. *Chilli con carne* is probably the world's best known example of the use of chillies. Numerous other Latin American meat, poultry and egg dishes are flavoured with chillies, as are fish and seafood. Similarly, chillies play an important part in much authentic Caribbean cooking (the traditional Trinidadian Pepperpot stew or Jamaican Pepperpot soup), and in the Creole food of the southern USA. Again, in many parts of Africa and the Middle East, chillies feature in all kinds of savoury dishes, as they do in India, where they are often included in the ginger and garlic paste used for meat cooking. See also: CAYENNE (p 65), PAPRIKA (p 87).

CINNAMON

Cinnamomum zeylanicum

Cinnamon grows in many tropical areas, including its native Sri Lanka, southern India, Indian Ocean islands like the Seychelles, Brazil and the West Indies. The tropical cinnamon evergreen can reach a height of 9 m (30 feet) or more, but it is from its young cultivated shoots that bark is harvested. The dried bark is eventually sold as a spice, in small quills usually 7.5-15 cm (3-6 inches) long, or as a powder.

Uses: Cinnamon is a universally popular spice, but as a very general rule it is used to flavour sweet dishes in the West and savoury ones in the East. In India cinnamon is an important flavouring in curries, *biryanis* and *kormas*. Indonesian *gulés* (curries) include it and it is popular in China too. In the Middle East and Greece cinnamon is used in both spicy meat stuffings for baked aubergines and courgettes and in nutty, honeyed fillings for pastries. Many European cakes and puddings, especially those featuring apples, include it.

CLOVES

Eugenia caryophyllus

The clove tree grows abundantly near tropical sea shores; an evergreen which can reach 13.5 m (45 feet), it is highly aromatic, its pungent scent being carried for miles by sea breezes. Cloves are the tree's immature, unopened flower buds, picked when turning from pale green to a pinkish-red. They dry to a rich deep brown and resemble small nail tacks in shape. Cloves are indigenous to the Moluccas or 'Spice Islands' of Indonesia, but cultivation is now widespread in the West Indies, Zanzibar, and all coastal regions of East Africa, Malaysia and Indonesia.

Cloves are both sweet and pungent with an unmistakable aroma, but use them with restraint to avoid overwhelming other tastes.

Uses: Like cinnamon, cloves feature in both sweet and savoury dishes and in an endless number of international spice mixtures. European stocks and soups often contain a couple of cloves and a single clove makes an interesting addition to a bouquet garni. In traditional British cooking, a clove or two should flavour bread sauce, and they should be used to stud the outside of a 'honey roast' ham. They blend well with apples in pies and crumbles and should be included in mulled wines and liqueurs.

CORIANDER SEEDS

Coriandrum sativum

Coriander is a member of the parsley family and grows in Asia, the Americas, Africa and Europe. The plant gives off a strong odour which disappears when the seeds are dried, to be replaced by a sweet, orangey aroma. Coriander seeds are almost completely round and look like tiny ridged brown footballs. Buy them whole from any good grocer or Indian store. The seeds are much milder than many other spices, so can be used in comparatively large quantities. The taste is fresh and mild with a hint of bitterness.

Uses: Indian curries, Indonesian *gulés*, and numerous other spicy dishes almost invariably include coriander seeds, and ground coriander is an ingredient in garam masala and other spice mixtures. In Western food, coriander seeds make an appearance in *à la grecque* dishes, pickling spice and in smoked meats and sausages, such as the Italian Mortadella. Coriander seeds are also popular in fish, chicken and game dishes. See also: CORIANDER (p 19).

CUMIN SEEDS
Cuminum cyminum

Like coriander, with which it is almost invariably paired in cooking, and caraway, which it closely resembles, cumin seed comes from a plant of the parsley family. A small and delicate annual, it is usually about 25 cm (10 inches) high. Native to the Middle East, cumin now grows in most hot climates: India, North Africa, China and the Americas. The spicy seeds are small, boat-shaped, ridged and greenish-brown in colour; they have a strong and unmistakable aroma, sweetish and warming. Their flavour is similarly pungent and penetrating, and they should be used in moderation.

Uses: In India, most savoury spice mixtures and curry seasonings feature cumin seeds, as do Indonesian mutton *gulés*, Thai and Malaysian fish and chicken curries and *satés*. In the Middle East and North Africa cumin flavours fish dishes, casseroles and couscous.

DILL SEEDS

Anethum graveolens

The dill plant is a member of the parsley family and the leaves and stalks, as well as the dried seeds, can all be used in cooking. A small, ridged oval in shape and light brown in colour, the seeds are flat on one side, rounded on the other. They have a fresh, sweet aroma but a slightly bitter taste, somewhat similar to caraway seeds. Use them whole or lightly crushed and add to dishes towards the end of cooking, or once cooking is over, to best preserve their flavour.

Uses: Dill seeds are particularly associated with the cookery of northern climes, although both seeds and leaves are popular in Sri Lanka. They can be a convenient substitute for the fresh herb, and can be used instead of fennel, although dill has a much milder flavour. The seeds are good in pickled dishes, vinegars, marinades and dressings, as well as in fresh and braised cucumber dishes and winter salads of potatoes or shredded root vegetables. In Russia and Scandinavia dill is a 'basic' seasoning and features in pickling mixtures for fish, as well as in creamy soups and sauces. It is also much used in chicken and vegetable dishes. See also: DILL (p 22).

FENNEL SEEDS

Foeniculum vulgare

Fennel is best known in Europe, especially around the Mediterranean, as a herb, salad ingredient and vegetable, but its dried seeds are also valuable in cooking. Like dill and anise, fennel is a member of the parsley family. The seeds — curved, ridged and dullish yellowgreen — are like plumper and larger versions of anise seeds.

Uses: Fennel seeds can often be used if the fresh herb is unavailable, and are a component of a number of spice mixtures. Fennel seeds are universally used with fish. In the West they are used in marinades, sauces and stuffings, or scattered over oily fish like mackerel and sardines before grilling. In India, Malaysia and Indonesia, they are used in fish curries. In both the West (especially Italy) and the East fennel seeds also have a traditional affinity with pork and poultry. See also: FENNEL (p 24).

FENUGREEK

Trigonella foenum-graecum

The 30-60 cm (1-2 foot) high fenugreek plant belongs to the bean and pea family; its flowers and pods resemble those of the pea. Each long, narrow pod contains ten to twenty ochre-brown seeds which resemble tiny pebbles both in appearance and texture. Native to the eastern Mediterranean and India, fenugreek has grown wild and in cultivation in Europe, Africa and Asia for thousands of years. Only when roasted do the seeds give off their pungent aroma; their taste is bitter-sweet and powerful so they should be used in moderation. Fenugreek seeds are easy to come by. Roast the whole seeds lightly until just golden, then grind to a powder. Ready-ground powder is also available.

Uses: Fenugreek is used most frequently in Indian food. Most curry powders include it, both commercial and home-prepared. A wide variety of spicy vegetable and pulse dishes feature fenugreek, which is often used in conjunction with fennel seeds. It is used in *halva*, the sesame-based sweetmeat found in India and Greece.

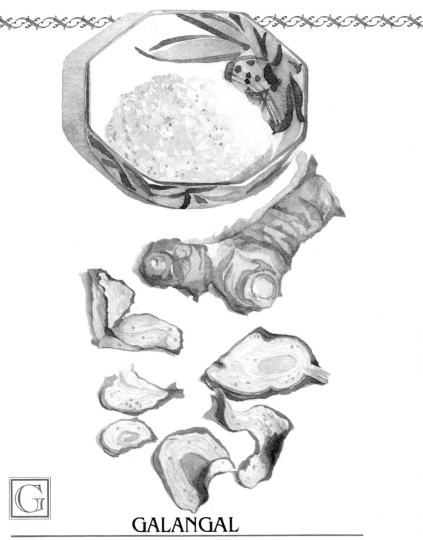

GALANGAL

Languas galanga
Languas officinarum
Kaempferia galanga

The tropical galangals are members of the same family as ginger, with which they have much in common both in form and flavour: it is their gingery-tasting and ginger-like rhizomes that are used in cooking. Greater galangal's knobbly rhizomes are orange-brown outside, yellow-white inside; Lesser's are rusty brown outside and a paler brown inside; Kaempferia's are reddish outside and white inside. The galangals grow in Indonesia, South-East Asia and southern China; they are a predominant spice in the cooking of Indonesia, Malaysia, Thailand and Indo-China. Ask for them by their local names in stores which stock Indonesian or Malaysian products: *laos* or *lengkuas* for Greater Galangal, *kencur* for Lesser, which has the most powerful flavour, and *kentjur* for Kaempferia, which is sweeter-tasting. The fresh rhizomes are not obtainable in the UK although the dried root is available in sliced or powder form.

Uses: Like ginger, galangal frequently features in fish and seafood dishes of Indonesia and Malaysia, whether fiery or delicately aromatic, and in spicy chicken, egg and vegetable dishes from the same areas. See also GINGER (p 78).

GINGER

Zingiber officinale

In its many forms, ginger is an important spice in both East and West. Like other tropical plants of the same family, such as the galangals and turmeric, it is the rhizome or knobbly root of the ginger plant which is used as a culinary spice. Fresh ginger root, essential for the exotic cuisines of many Eastern lands, is easily acquired. It is very different from dried ginger and the latter cannot be used as a substitute for it in Asian dishes. Dried ginger root, similarly, comes whole, in pieces or slices; it is sold in two forms: 'black' with its outer layer intact, or 'white' without. It is prepared from the tougher, more fibrous parts nearer the root and must be firmly bruised with a hammer or similar instrument before use to break up the fibres. The beige powder sold commercially is the dried ground root.

Uses: Ginger is one of the most widely used spices, though certain of its forms and uses are more popular in certain areas; the broadest division being between its use in sweet dishes in the West and savoury ones in the East. In Asia and the East fresh ginger is used in numerous savoury dishes of meat, poultry and fish, while thin, delicate slices of pickled ginger (preserved in brine or vinegar) are a favourite side dish or garnish in China and Japan. Ground dried ginger is an important and traditional baking and pudding spice in the West. See also: GINGER (p 28).

JUNIPER BERRIES

Juniperus communis

A small coniferous and prickly evergreen, the juniper tree ranges in height from 120 cm-10.5 m (4-35 feet) and grows throughout Europe. The small spherical berries turn from an unripe green to a ripe blue-black; when dried, they are a purplish-black and light brown inside. The berries' spicy pine aroma and sweet, resinous flavour varies according to where they grow; those from southern regions are far more pungent than the northern varieties.

Uses: Juniper berries have a particular affinity with robust meat dishes, and can be included in marinades and stuffings for game, pork and poultry and in hearty beef stews. Traditionally used in English spiced salt beef and in the curing of Welsh and York hams, juniper berries feature in many other traditional European salted meats as well as in pâtés, terrines and potted meats.

KOKUM

Garcinia indica

The solitary tall and slender kokum tree grows exclusively along the paradise-like coast of tropical south-western India; related to the mangosteen, it can reach a height of 15 m (50 feet). Its round, purplish, plum-like fruit contains eight seeds, but it is the skin of the fruit that is used in cooking. Stripped from the fruit, flattened and dried, the skins turn a deep black-brown and have a sour and rather salty taste; like tamarind, with which it has much in common, kokum is often used as a souring agent. Kokum may be bought from good Indian grocers and should be kept in an airtight container, for use according to recipe instructions: either whole or as an infused liquid.

Uses: Kokum is a uniquely Indian flavouring, used especially in its native region. Fresh fish and seafood abound, and three or four skins are often included in marinades for grills and kebabs, in curries and other spiced fish dishes. Like tamarind and amchur, kokum is also used in fresh tangy chutneys, pickles and butters.

MACE

Myristica fragrans

Mace and nutmeg are two completely distinct but uniquely related spices: they are both parts of the fruit of a towering tropical evergreen tree which grows in the Moluccas and the rest of Indonesia, the Philippines, Malaysia and the Caribbean. Mace is the crimson, lacy 'cage' at the centre of the fruit which encloses a dark brown shell containing the seed or kernel (nutmeg). When the fruit is harvested, the mace is removed from the nutmeg, flattened and dried in the sun to become hard and brittle, ochre-orange, 2.5-4 cm (1-1½ inch) long blades. Mace is available both as blades and ready-ground, although ground mace deteriorates rapidly.

Uses: Mace tastes and smells rather like nutmeg but is much more powerful and should be used in moderation. Because of its warm pungency, mace is best suited to savoury dishes; use the blades in sauces, soups, chowders and casseroles and other liquids from which they can be removed after cooking. Like nutmeg, ground mace can also be used to boost sweet dishes, particularly milk puddings. See also: NUTMEG (p 86).

MUSTARD

fam. Cruciferae

Mustard is a condiment prepared from the seeds of three plants of the cabbage family. There are three types of seeds: White, Brown and Black, and the huge number of different mustards available are based on combinations of these three seed types, blended with other flavouring ingredients such as wine, vinegar, allspice, pepper-corns, tarragon, chillies and garlic. Most supermarkets sell a basic range of mustards, but for a more `exotic range look in delicatessens and quality grocery shops.

Prepared mustards will keep for about 6 months in airtight jars. Powders will keep for 3-4 months in tins. Remember that mustard's pungency is destroyed by heat, so for a fiery result it should be added to sauces or stews after the cooking is finished.

All mustards are highly effective in bringing out the flavour of most meats, particularly beef, pork and game. Many cheese, egg and vegetable dishes can also benefit from the use of mustard.

English mustard is a combination of white and black mustard seeds, wheat flour and turmeric – which gives it its familiar yellow colour. Mustard powder should be mixed with cold water and left for 15 minutes to develop its fiery flavour, a milder flavour can be achieved by mixing the powder with milk or cream and a drop of sugar. Ready mixed English mustard is not as strong as the freshly prepared kind. The hot sharpness of English mustard combines as a condiment with simple strong-tasting fare such as sharp Cheddar cheese, country sausages, roast beef, pork and gammon.

Bordeaux mustard consists of black mustard seeds blended with unfermented claret, often flavoured with herbs especially tarragon. Dark brown and aromatic, it has a mild sweet/sour taste and is the connoisseur's choice to accompany grilled steaks and cold meats.

Dijon mustard from Burgundy is made from husked black seeds blended with salt, spices and white wine or verjuice — an acid juice made from unripe green grapes. Many varieties are available, but all are a palish grey-yellow colour with a subtle flavour which varies in pungency from mild to very hot. Dijon mustards are used in preference to any other type in delicate classic sauces such as Cumberland, devil and *remoulade*.

Meaux mustard is a mixture of crushed and ground black seeds mixed with vinegar and spices. Many varieties are available but the most popular is sold in wide-mouthed stoneware jars, the cork secured with red sealing wax. Meaux mustards have an unusual crunchy texture and a fairly hot flavour. They make a good accompaniment to cold meats and hams.

German mustard is a combination of strong black mustard flour and vinegar. Smooth, slightly sweet and aromatic, it is less pungent than English mustard but more so than Bordeaux. German mustard is often flavoured with herbs, especially tarragon, and is best partnered with the various types of sausage popular in that country — *knackwurst, bockwurst* and so on.

American mustard is made from white mustard seeds, white wine, sugar and vinegar. It is pale yellow, mild and sweet and has a smooth sauce-like consistency. It makes a good accompaniment for hot dogs and hamburgers and can be spread lightly over chops before grilling. See also MUSTARD SEEDS (p 84).

MUSTARD SEEDS

Brassica nigra
Brassica juncea
Brassica alba

Whole mustard seeds are the basis of all prepared mustards, and the pungent mustard oil, much used in India, is extracted from them; they are also used as a cooking spice, especially in India and neighbouring countries. Though there are three main varieties of mustard plants, Black, Brown (or Indian), and White, all three plants are similar in looks and grow to about 75-105 cm (2½-3½ feet); all bear tiny, spherical, hard seeds contained in long pods. Mustard is an important commercial crop in many areas of the world, but it is the seeds of Brown mustard that are the typical Indian cooking spice. If used raw, in pickling for instance, mustard seeds are powerfully hot, but if they are fried quickly in hot oil before use their pungency diminishes and they become deliciously sweet and nutty. They are easily acquired from Asian grocers.

Uses: Mustard seeds are used primarily in Indian food, but the White variety are sometimes used in the West, as a component of pickling spice, for example. The Brown seeds are used in a wide range of Indian, Sri Lankan and Malaysian dishes, and they blend well with other spices. Used raw they flavour pickles and chutneys. Whole and roasted, they are best known for their successful partnership with vegetables. See also: MUSTARD (p 82).

NIGELLA SEEDS

Nigella sativa

The nigella plant, which grows to about 60 cm (2 feet), is a small herbaceous annual of the buttercup family. Nigella grows wild and in cultivation in parts of central and southern Europe and Asia; it is also cultivated in the Middle East and extensively in India. Its tiny black teardrop seeds, rough on the outside and oily white inside, are used as a cooking spice. The seeds' earthy aroma, faint until they are rubbed or bruised, is slightly reminiscent of carrots or nutmeg and they are peppery and crunchy to taste.

Uses: Nigella seeds are important in the cookery of India and the Middle East. Often lightly roasted before use, they play the role of both spice and condiment, their peppery flavour making them an ideal pepper substitute. They give flavour and texture to bread doughs, cakes and patries.

NUTMEG

Myristica fragrans

The nutmeg kernel is dried in its seedcoat, which is then removed. Oval in shape and about 4 cm (1½ inches) long, the nutmeg has a hard, brown, uneven surface and a paler interior. Nutmeg is milder than mace but has a similar though more nutty flavour; warm and sweetish, it also has a light bitter undertone.

Uses: Nutmeg is widely used in both Western and Eastern cooking. In India and South-East Asia it is an important meat seasoning; in the West it features in sweet and savoury dishes alike. It harmonizes with other spices, and enhances and blends with a wide variety of flavours. Like mace, nutmeg is a traditional ingredient of English pies and puddings, such as steak, kidney and oyster pudding, baked custard and junket. See also: MACE (p 81).

PAPRIKA

Capsicum annuum

Brick-red paprika is a very familiar spice in the West, especially in Spain and Hungary. Like cayenne pepper, it is a finely ground powder made from the fruits of several different chilli plants. The ripe flesh is used for mild and sweet paprikas; for more pungent versions the seeds are included. Paprika chillies are widely grown in Spain as well as in a number of eastern European countries and the USA. Both Spain and Hungary (where paprika is considered the national spice) produce several types, graded according to quality and pungency. The mildest kind is best known and most widely sold in Britain, it has a light, sweet smell and almost no pungency; the most pungent paprika is as powerful as cayenne. All paprikas impart a wonderful rich, reddish-brown colour to food.

Uses: In Hungary, paprika flavours a profusion of savoury foods — from meat stews, such as goulash, fish and poultry to vegetables, cheeses and soured cream. Paprika is particularly good with fish and shellfish. See also: CAYENNE (p 65), CHILLI (p 67).

PEPPER

Piper nigrum

Pepper is undoubtedly the most familiar and indispens-
able of all cooking spices in the West. It comes from the
tropical trailing vines of the Piperaceae family. Native to
southern India and South-East Asia, pepper vines are
now cultivated in many tropical areas such as Brazil, the
East and West Indies, Indonesia and Malaysia. The vines
grow to heights of 3.6 m (12 feet) and bear long 'strings'
of 20-30 small berries which ripen from green to
reddish-yellow. Black peppercorns are the dried, unripe
berries of the Piper nigrum vine; white peppercorns are
the riper red berries, washed, fermented, de-husked and
dried; green peppercorns are the fresh, unripe berries,
pickled or freeze-dried. Black pepper is stronger than
white, while green peppercorns have a milder, fresh
taste.
Uses: Pepper is a universal seasoning and condiment.
Whole or crushed peppercorns are an important component in a wide range of spice mixtures and whole
peppercorns are frequently added to marinades, stocks
and *court bouillons*. Fresh green peppercorns are used
to make sauces to serve with both fish and chicken.
Roughly ground or crushed peppercorns are important
charcuterie seasonings.

POPPY SEEDS

Papaver somniferum

The pretty opium poppy is the source not only of a highly narcotic drug but also of the harmless and delicious poppy seeds used in cooking. The plant is related to both the common field poppy and garden varieties. It grows to anything from 30-120 cm (1-4 feet) and bears white, pink or lilac flowers and erect oval seedpods which contain a mass of hard, minuscule seeds. The lilac-flowered Asian variety has creamy-coloured seeds, while those of the European variety are blue-grey. Both types are very mild and sweetish and acquire a bitter-sweet, nutty flavour when cooked.

Uses: Blue-grey poppy seeds are most commonly used in the West and the creamy version in the East, but they can be interchanged without alteration of flavour. In the West, poppy seed is best known for its association with baking; it is especially popular in Poland and Germany, and in traditional Jewish baking. In the East, poppy seeds are used in India and Japan (where their oil is popular too), either whole in a variety of vegetable dishes and chutneys, or crushed or ground in certain varieties of spice mixtures for *kormas*, *masalas* and tandooris.

S

SAFFRON

Crocus sativus

Saffron is the world's most expensive spice and unique in its origin, for saffron is the dried stigmas of the flowers of the saffron crocus. The stigmas are extracted from the freshly harvested flowers and dried to become irregular, deep orange-red threads about 4 cm (1½ inches) long. It takes about 50,000 stigmas to make up 100 g (4 oz) saffron, and every bloom must be individually packed, and every stigma individually extracted by hand. Saffron flourishes in the hot but not tropical climates of the south of France, the Middle East, Kashmir and China; the best saffron is said to come from Valencia in Spain. It imparts a distinctive aroma, a bitter, honey-like taste and a strong, yellow colour to food. Buy threads in preference to powder, which can easily be tampered with.

Uses: To use saffron, either infuse a few threads in a cup of hot water and add the coloured liquid towards the end of cooking, or crumble the threads and add directly to the pot. Alternatively, dry roast, crumble and then steep the crumbled threads as done in India. Ready-ground powder can be added directly to the pot. Saffron is important in the cooking of Spain and other Mediterranean countries, the Middle East and India: in all these areas it is particularly associated with rice dishes, both savoury and sweet.

SASSAFRAS

Sassafras albidum

Sassafras is one of the few true North American spices, well known to the indigenous American Indians. The sassafras tree grows to a height of 13 m (43 feet); its flowers are yellow and its berries dark blue. It is a common wayside tree, of which the aromatic leaves, roots, root bark, pith and shoots are used as a spicy flavouring. In cookery, the leaves are generally the most important: these are dried and powdered to form what is known as *filé* powder. Look for proprietary brands of *filé* powder at specialist spice suppliers.

Uses: Sassafras is primarily associated with the exotic, highly seasoned Creole cooking of the American 'deep south'. Here, *filé* powder appears in soups, sauces, meat and fish stews and casseroles, and especially *gumbo*, a thick soup or stew of okra, sweet peppers, onions, tomatoes and chillies served with rice. The shoots, roots and sassafras oil are used in traditional sassafras cordials, beers and other bottled and carbonated drinks.

SESAME SEEDS

Sesamum indicum

Sesame is a tropical annual with a pungent smell and foxglove-like flowers. The sesame plant grows to anything between 60-180 cm (2-6 feet), and its seedpods contain a large number of small, flat, oval seeds in a variety of colours; the most commonly on sale are black and beige (unhulled) or white (hulled and polished). Sesame is native to India, but it is also grown extensively in the hot climates of Africa, parts of the Americas, China and the Middle East. Dried sesame seeds have a mildly nutty aroma and a stronger nutty flavour and are widely available. Dry roast before use or fry lightly in a little oil until they just turn colour, begin to jump and give off a roasted aroma.

Uses: Sesame seeds are popular in both Chinese and Japanese cooking, in which their nutty oil is a favourite flavouring. In Indian cookery, sesame seeds flavour aubergines and beans, and make deliciously nutty fried potato dishes and potato salads. In their crushed, ground form, sesame seeds are well known as the cream paste, *tahini*.

STAR ANISE

Illicium verum

Star anise is an attractive oriental spice, especially associated with Chinese cookery. It is the dried fruit of an oriental evergreen of the magnolia family which can reach a height of 7.3 m (24 feet) and is a native of China and Japan, where it still mainly grows, though it is also established in parts of Indo-China and the Philippines. Harvested when unripe and dried in the sun, each reddish-brown, star-shaped fruit contains 8 small, brown, oval seeds. The dried stars have a pungent but harsh aniseed aroma and are available whole or ready-ground from good grocers, especially those which stock Chinese provisions.

Uses: Star anise is an important component in spice mixtures, Chinese and Malay curry mixtures (which are 'sweeter' than Indian ones), and in some Chinese spiced salts. Like other aniseed-flavoured spices, star anise combines excellently with fish, and it can be used instead of Pernod in Western fish dishes and sauces for fish and shellfish.

SUMAC

Rhus coriaria

Sumac grows wild in many rugged regions of the Middle East and all round the Mediterranean, but its use as a spice and souring agent, as opposed to a dye or tanning aid, is mainly confined to Levantine or Arabic food. A robust shrub with hairy leaves and branches, which grows to about 3 m (10 feet), it bears clusters of deep-red, hairy berries which, when dried, are used in cooking, mainly as a souring agent. Not surprisingly, it has a sour but fruity, astringent taste. The rough, deep reddish-purple powder made from the dried berries, which can be added directly to the cooking pot, is usually available in shops which stock Middle Eastern, Lebanese or Jewish groceries. Whole berries, if these can be acquired, should be crushed, steeped in hot water and then squeezed and the extracted juice used like lemon juice.

Uses: In its extracted juice form sumac is used extensively as a dressing for salads and as a marinade for meat, poultry and fish, especially when barbecued.

TURMERIC

Curcuma longa

With its spiky yellow flowers and long, shiny, pointed leaves, the tropical turmeric can reach a height of 1 m (3½ feet) and grows profusely in the tropical climates of many parts of the world – from India and the Far East to Africa and Latin America. It is a typical member of the ginger family, and like both ginger and galangal, it is the rhizomes, or knobbly roots, which form the cooking spice. It has a strong woody aroma and distinctive, pungent flavour.

Uses: Turmeric is used for flavour and colour in Malaysian, Indonesian, Indian and Middle Eastern food; it is best known for its partnership with fish and rice, and its inclusion in numerous curried dishes. Most Indian curry powder mixes for both 'wet' and 'dry' dishes feature turmeric, as do *korma* and other spice mixtures. In addition, it is frequently added to pulse dishes like *dhal*, and used as a condiment with vegetables. Certain festive rice dishes take their colour from turmeric as opposed to saffron, and it is a must in the traditional English kedgeree.

LIST OF SUPPLIERS

Nowadays herb plants are fairly easy to obtain, but if you have problems obtaining any of the herbs mentioned in this book, it might be worth contacting the following suppliers, all of whom operate a mail order service.

Herb plants and seeds.
Send S.A.E. for list.

Hollington Nurseries,
Woolton Hill,
Newbury,
Berkshire
Tel: Highclere 253908

Herb seeds.
Catalogue on request.

Suttons Seeds Ltd,
Hele Road,
Torquay,
Devon,
TQ2 7QJ

Herb plants and seeds.
Send S.A.E. for list.

Ashfields Herb Nursery,
Henstock,
Market Drayton,
Salop TF9 2NG
Tel: 095 279 392

Herb seeds.
Catalogue on request.

Down to Earth Seeds,
Streetfield Farm,
Cade Street,
Heathfield,
East Sussex,
TN21 9BS
Tel: 04352 3964

Herb plants.
Send S.A.E. for list (no callers).

Lighthorne Associates Ltd,
Moreton Morrell,
Warwick CU35 9DB